JOHN STOTT BIB[LE]
13 Studi[es]

Jesus Christ

Teacher, Servant & Savior

John
STOTT

with Dale and Sandy Larsen

Inter-Varsity Press
Nottingham, England

IVP Connect
An imprint of InterVarsity Press
Downers Grove, Illinois

InterVarsity Press, USA
P.O. Box 1400, Downers Grove, IL 60515-1426, USA
World Wide Web: www.ivpress.com
Email: email@ivpress.com

Inter-Varsity Press, England
Norton Street, Nottingham NG7 3HR, England
Website: www.ivpbooks.com
Email: ivp@ivpbooks.com

InterVarsity Press®, USA, is the book-publishing division of InterVarsity Christian Fellowship/USA®,
a student movement active on campus at hundreds of universities, colleges and schools of nursing in
the United States of America, and a member movement of the International Fellowship of Evangelical
Students. For information about local and regional activities, write Public Relations Dept., InterVarsity
Christian Fellowship/USA, 6400 Schroeder Rd., P.O. Box 7895, Madison, WI 53707-7895, or visit the IVCF
website at <www.intervarsity.org>.

Inter-Varsity Press, England, is closely linked with the Universities and Colleges Christian Fellowship, a
student movement connecting Christian Unions in universities and colleges throughout Great Britain, and
a member movement of the International Fellowship of Evangelical Students. Website: www.uccf.org.uk.

This study guide is based on and includes excerpts adapted from The Incomparable Christ ©2001 by John
R. W. Stott.

Design: Cindy Kiple
Images: Allan Brown/iStockphoto

USA ISBN 978-0-8308-2022-1
UK ISBN 978-1-84474-323-0

Printed in the United States of America ∞

P   21   20   19   18   17   16   15   14   13   12   11   10   9   8   7   6   5

Y   25   24   23   22   21   20   19   18   17   16   15   14   13   12

Introducing Jesus Christ

For twenty centuries Jesus Christ has been the dominant figure in Western culture.

Jesus is *the center of history*. A large proportion of the human race continues to divide history into B.C. and A.D. by reference to his birth. In the year 2000 the world population reached 6 billion, while the estimated number of Christians was 1.7 billion, or about 28 percent. So nearly one third of the human race professes to follow Jesus.

Jesus is *the focus of Scripture*. The Bible is not a random collection of religious documents. As Jesus himself said, "The Scriptures . . . bear witness to me" (John 5:39 RSV). And Christian scholars have always recognized this.

Jesus is *the heart of mission*. Why is it that some Christians cross land and sea, continents and cultures, as missionaries? It is in order to commend not a civilization, an institution or an ideology, but rather a person, Jesus Christ, whom they believe to be unique. Those who see Jesus and surrender to him acknowledge him as the center of their conversion experience.

In these studies we will explore the Christ of the New Testament witness. We begin in Matthew by exploring how Jesus is the fulfillment of the Old Testament. Then we move through the gospels and the letters discovering different aspects of Christ in each book. The testimony of the New Testament to Jesus is both rich in its diversity, and, at the same time, recognizedly, a united witness.

My hope and prayer is that these studies will reveal Jesus Christ as the proper object of our worship, witness and hope, and as deserving the description *incomparable*. For he has neither rivals nor peers.

Suggestions for Individual Study

1. As you begin each study, pray that God will speak to you through his Word.

2. Read the introduction to the study and respond to the questions that follow it. This is designed to help you get into the theme of the study.

3. The studies are written in an inductive format designed to help you discover for yourself what Scripture is saying. Each study deals with a particular passage so that you can really delve into the author's meaning in that context. Read and reread the passage to be studied. The questions are written using the language of the New International Version, so you may wish to use that version of the Bible. The New Revised Standard Version is also recommended.

4. Each study includes three types of questions. *Observation* questions ask about the basic facts: who, what, when, where and how. *Interpretation* questions delve into the meaning of the passage. *Application* questions (also found in the "Apply" section) help you discover the implications of the text for growing in Christ. These three keys unlock the treasures of Scripture.

Write your answers to the study questions in the spaces provided or in a personal journal. Writing can bring clarity and deeper understanding of yourself and of God's Word.

5. In the studies you will find some commentary notes designed to give help with complex verses by giving further biblical and cultural background and contextual information. The notes in the studies are not designed to answer the questions for you. They are to help you along as you learn to study the Bible for yourself. This guide is based on part one of John Stott's book *The Incomparable Christ*.

6. Move to the "Apply" section. These questions will help you connect the key biblical themes to your own life. Putting the application into practice is one of the keys to growing in Christ.

7. Use the guidelines in the "Pray" section to focus on God, thanking him for what you have learned and praying about the applications that have come to mind.

Suggestions for Members of a Group Study

1. Come to the study prepared. Follow the suggestions for individual study mentioned above. You will find that careful preparation will greatly enrich your time spent in group discussion.

2. Be willing to participate in the discussion. The leader of your group will not be lecturing. Instead, she or he will be encouraging the members of the group to discuss what they have learned. The leader will be asking the questions that are found in this guide.

3. Stick to the topic being discussed. Your answers should be based on the verses which are the focus of the discussion and not on outside authorities such as commentaries or speakers. These studies focus on a particular passage of Scripture. Only rarely should you refer to other portions of the Bible. This allows for everyone to participate on equal ground and for in-depth study.

4. Be sensitive to the other members of the group. Listen attentively when they describe what they have learned. You may be surprised by their insights! Each question assumes a variety of answers. Many questions do not have "right" answers, particularly questions that aim at meaning or application. Instead the questions push us to explore the passage more thoroughly.

When possible, link what you say to the comments of others. Also, be affirming whenever you can. This will encourage some of the more hesitant members of the group to participate.

5. Be careful not to dominate the discussion. We are sometimes so eager to express our thoughts that we leave too little opportunity for others to respond. By all means participate! But allow others to also.

6. Expect God to teach you through the passage being discussed and through the other members of the group. Pray that you will have an enjoyable and profitable time together, but also that as a result of the study you will find ways that you can take action individually and/or as a group.

7. It will be helpful for groups to follow a few basic guidelines. These guidelines, which you may wish to adapt to your situation, should be read at the beginning of the first session.

☐ Anything said in the group is considered confidential and will not be discussed outside the group unless specific permission is given to do so.

☐ We will provide time for each person present to talk if he or she feels comfortable doing so.

☐ We will talk about ourselves and our own situations, avoiding conversation about other people.

☐ We will listen attentively to each other.

☐ We will be very cautious about giving advice.

8. If you are the group leader, you will find additional suggestions at the back of the guide.

1
FULFILLMENT
OF SCRIPTURE

Matthew 1:1-17;
5:17-20; 21:28-45

*T*he major feature of Jesus, according to the Gospel of Matthew, can be stated in one word: *fulfillment*. Strongly Jewish in his origin and culture, Matthew portrays Jesus as the fulfillment of the Old Testament. Matthew's Gospel serves as a bridge between the two Testaments, between preparation and fulfillment. The Old Testament prophets lived in the period of anticipation; the apostles were living in the time of fulfillment.

Open
■ What sorts of things are worth waiting for? What makes them worth the wait?

Study
■ *Read Matthew 1:1-17.* Matthew does not portray Jesus as another prophet, one more seer in the succession of the centuries, but rather as

the fulfillment of all prophecy. It was in and with the ministry of Jesus that the long-awaited kingdom of God had come. First, then, Matthew's Christ was the *fulfillment of prophecy.*

1. What familiar names do you find in Jesus' genealogy?

2. Matthew traces Jesus' lineage back to Abraham, the father of the cho-sen people, through whom God promised to bless the world (1:2). What significance do you see in Jesus being descended from Abraham?

3. Matthew also traces Jesus' lineage back to David, the greatest of Is-rael's kings, who was the exemplar of the great king to come (1:6). What significance do you see in Jesus being descended from David?

Summary: In his Gospel, Matthew's favorite formula is "Now this took place that it might be fulfilled which was written." This phrase occurs eleven times. His intention is to demonstrate that everything that has happened has been predicted and that everything that has been pre-dicted has been fulfilled.

Matthew's Christ is also *the fulfillment of the law,* that is, the Old Testament law given by God. Jesus seemed to his contemporaries to be disrespectful of the law; he seemed to be lax where they were strict. But Jesus insisted that he was loyal to the law. *Read Matthew 5:17-20.*

4. How does Jesus emphasize the vital importance of the law?

---

5. Put yourself in the place of one of Jesus' disciples hearing him say these remarkable words. You have always thought of the Pharisees and the teachers of the law (5:20) as the most righteous people on Earth. What do you make of Jesus' words?

Summary: Christian righteousness is greater than Pharisaic righteousness, because it is deeper. It is a righteousness of the heart, a righteousness not of words and deeds only but especially of thoughts and motives (see 5:21-30). It is in this sense that Jesus is the fulfillment of the law. He takes it to its logical conclusion. He looks beyond a superficial understanding of the law to its radical demand for heart righteousness.

Matthew's Christ is *the fulfillment of Israel.* This is the most subtle of the three fulfillments. Matthew sees Jesus confronting Israel with a final summons to repent. Later, Jesus' great commission would open the apostles' horizons to the Gentile world; now, however, during his earthly ministry, Israel is to be given one more chance. But they persist in their rebellion. *Read Matthew 21:28-45.*

---

6. Jesus tells two parables in this passage. His audience is a delegation of Jewish chief priests and elders (21:23). What message does the first parable hold for them (21:28-32)?

7. How do you think Jesus' hearers react to his strong statement in Matthew 21:31-32?

8. What is the point of Jesus' second parable (21:33-44)?

9. How does Jesus place himself in the second parable (21:37-39)?

10. On what basis do you think the chief priests and Pharisees "knew he was talking about them" when they heard these parables (21:45)?

Summary: Jesus sees himself as the sole surviving representative of authentic Israel. He alone remains faithful; otherwise the whole nation has become apostate. At the same time, he is the beginning of a new Israel. The kingdom of God will be transferred (21:43) to his people, whom he calls his "church," a countercultural community characterized by the values and standards of his kingdom, as described in the Sermon on the Mount.

Apply————————————————————
■ What has been your attitude toward the Old Testament? How has it changed or developed over the years?

How is your attitude toward or understanding of the Old Testament affected by the knowledge that Jesus Christ is its complete fulfillment?

If you are not familiar with Old Testament prophecy or law or the purposes of Israel, what steps will you take to familiarize yourself?

On a personal level, how has Jesus shown himself to be the fulfillment of your needs and hopes?

Pray

■ Thank God that he has not left anything undone but has fulfilled all his promises in Christ. Ask him to make you even more aware of the complete sufficiency of Christ.

2
SUFFERING
SERVANT

Mark 8:27-38

*D*own through church history, the crucial questions have been christological. That is, they concern the identity, the mission and the demands of Jesus. If Matthew presents Jesus as the Christ of Scripture, Mark presents him as the Suffering Servant of the Lord, who dies for his people's sins. The cross is at the center of Mark's understanding of Jesus. Indeed one-third of Mark's whole Gospel is devoted to the story of the cross.

Open——————————————————————

■ What could be good about suffering?

When have you found joy in sacrificial service?

Study——————————————————————

■ *Read Mark 8:27-30.* Consider a crucial passage from Mark's Gospel, which brings together three of his favorite themes: who Jesus is, what he has come to do and what he requires of his followers. This text is a turning point in the Gospel because it shows a turning point in the ministry of Jesus. Before this incident Jesus has been fêted as a popular teacher and healer; from now on he warns his disciples of the coming cross.

---

1. Contrast the general public opinion about Jesus' identity with the opinion of the disciples (or at least Peter).

How do you account for the difference?

---

2. What importance do you attach to the question of who Jesus is?

Jesus knows there is a difference between the people's public perceptions of his identity and the apostles' private, dawning conviction. According to public opinion, he is John the Baptist, Elijah or another prophet; according to the Twelve, he is not another prophet but "the Christ," the fulfillment of all prophecy. Jesus' warning not to tell anyone about him (v. 30) has puzzled many readers. The reason is that the public had false political notions of the Messiah. Jesus is evidently afraid that the people would cast him in a revolutionary role; but he has not come to be a political messiah. He has, rather, come to die, and through death, to secure a spiritual liberation for his people.

---

3. *Read Mark 8:31-33.* What is Jesus' plain message to his disciples?

---

4. What two fierce reactions quickly follow?

5. Peter has the understandable desire to save Jesus from suffering and death. How can Jesus go to the extreme of equating Peter's resistance with the efforts of Satan (v. 33)?

Summary: Jesus speaks openly and plainly about what he has come to do; there is to be no secret about the kind of Messiah he has come to be. Hearing Jesus' prediction of the cross, Peter is brash enough to rebuke him, so Jesus turns and rebukes Peter. Nothing must be allowed to undermine the necessity of the cross.

6. *Read Mark 8:34-38.* How does Jesus' audience change at this point (v. 34)?

7. What paradoxes or apparent contradictions do you find in this passage?

8. Which of Jesus' statements in this passage strikes you as most difficult, and why?

Jesus moves at once from his cross to ours, and he portrays Christian discipleship in terms of self-denial and even death. Christian discipleship is much more radical than an amalgam of beliefs, good works and religious practices. No imagery can do it justice, except for death and resurrection. For when we lose ourselves we find ourselves, and when we die we live.

9. When have you experienced the truth of saving your life by losing it (v. 35)?

10. When have you paid a price (perhaps socially, financially, professionally or in some other way) for publicly professing your faith in Christ?

Summary: Here are three fundamental themes in the Gospel of Mark. *Who is Jesus?* The Christ. *What did he come to do?* To serve, to suffer and to die. *What does he ask of his disciples?* To take up our crosses and follow him through the death of self-denial into the glory of resurrection. There is no authentic Christian faith or life unless the cross is at the center.

Apply

■ In what areas are you still clinging to your own life, and with what expectations?

In what situations are you ashamed of Christ, not because of who he is but because of the possible cost of identifying yourself with him?

Pray

■ Thank the Lord that he did not take the easy route and give in to the pressure to escape the cross. Pray for his grace and strength to help you make the difficult choices that he places before you.

3
SAVIOR OF
THE WORLD

Luke 18:15—19:10

*L*uke is the only Gentile contributor to the New Testament. So it is entirely appropriate that he should present Jesus neither as the Christ of Scripture (as Matthew does) nor as the Suffering Servant (as Mark does), but as the Savior of the world, irrespective of race or nationality, rank, sex, need or age. The Christ of Luke's Gospel is the Savior of the world.

Open
■ When you reflect on God's love for all people, what people or groups of people might you think would be highly unlikely to respond to the Gospel? Why do you mentally exclude them?

Study
■ *Read Luke 18:15-17.* What is Luke's message? First, it is *good news of salvation. Salvation* is a key word in Luke's Gospel. Negatively, it is the removal of guilt (bringing forgiveness). Positively, it is the bestowal of the Holy Spirit (conveying new birth). Forgiveness eradicates our past, and the Spirit transforms our future. Moreover, this great salvation

brings joy. Second, Luke's message is good news of *salvation through Christ*. In no other person has God become human, died, been raised from death and been exalted to heaven, so there is no other savior, since no one else possesses his qualifications. Third, Luke's message is good news of salvation through Christ *for the whole world*. God's love in Christ encompasses everybody, especially those who are pushed to the margins of society.

1. Luke depicts Jesus as going out of his way to honor those the world despised, to befriend the friendless and to include the excluded. For example, in the ancient world women were generally despised and oppressed, and unwanted children were abandoned or killed. But Luke emphasizes that Jesus loved and respected both. Why do you think the disciples rebuke those who are bringing babies to Jesus?

2. Jesus welcomes the young children who are brought to him. How do you think his words and actions affect the watching parents?

3. What spiritual parallel does Jesus draw from the children?

4. Luke is more interested than the other Gospel writers with questions of wealth and poverty. He is concerned for economic equality and affirms that Jesus has been anointed "to preach good news to the poor" (Luke 4:18). *Read Luke 18:18-34.* The wealthy ruler is morally respectable (18:19-21) and has a worthy goal: eternal life (18:18). What problem does Jesus still discern within him (18:22)?

5. Why is it hard for the rich to enter the kingdom of God (18:23-27)?

6. Jesus promises certain compensations for those who make sacrifices for the kingdom of God (18:28-30). He then tells his disciples that he will be rejected and killed (18:31-34). How do you personally respond to what he says?

7. All four Gospel writers describe the healing ministry of Jesus, but Luke, the physician, shows a special interest in it. *Read Luke 18:35-44.* What contrasts do you find between how the onlookers respond to the blind man and how Jesus responds to him (18:35-41)?

8. Both the tax collectors and "sinners" who are spoken of are social outcasts: tax collectors because they are employed by the hated Romans and "sinners" because they are ignorant of Jewish laws and traditions. But Luke tells us that both tax collectors and sinners gather around Jesus (Luke 15:1), that in spite of criticism, Jesus eats with them (Luke 5:30; 15:2) and is nicknamed their friend (Luke 7:34). *Read Luke 19:1-10.* When Jesus visited Jericho, to what lengths did Zacchaeus go in order to get a glimpse of him (19:1-4)?

9. Why were people shocked at Jesus' response to Zacchaeus (19:5-7)?

10. The change in Zacchaeus's life is both rapid and radical. How do you respond when you read his words in verse 9? (Are you surprised? Skeptical?)

---

11. How does Jesus' statement in Luke 19:10 summarize this entire passage from Luke (18:15—19:10)?

Summary: These are the parameters of Luke's two-volume story in the Gospel and Acts: salvation (including both forgiveness and the Spirit), Christ (who by his birth, death and resurrection was uniquely competent to save) and the world he came to save, irrespective of ethnicity, class, sex, age or need. God's love in Christ encompasses everybody, especially those who are pushed to the margins of society. He reaches out to touch those that others regard as untouchable. Luke's Christ is the Savior of the world.

Apply————————————————————————————
■ When have you especially felt embraced by Christ even as others have excluded you?

When and how has God showed you that he loves those you might tend to exclude?

Who will you extend the love of Christ to this week?

Pray————————————————————————————
■ Thank the Lord for including you in his love and mercy. Ask his forgiveness for excluding or simply ignoring certain people, and pray for the courage to reach out to them in practical ways.

4
WORD MADE FLESH

John 1:1-14

*E*ach of the four Gospels has a different beginning. Matthew opens with Jesus' genealogy, tracing his family tree back to Abraham, and Luke with Jesus' conception, birth and infancy. Mark starts with the ministry of John the Baptist, while John goes right back to the beginning of time. The personal and eternal Word was also the agent of creation, who had never left the world he had made, and who is the light and life of all human beings.

Open————————————————————

■ Light, whether natural or artificial, is something most people take for granted. When have you been especially appreciative of light?

Study————————————————————

■ *Read John 1:1-5.* What was John's purpose in writing his Gospel? He tells us: "Jesus did many other miraculous signs in the presence of his disciples, which are not recorded in this book. But these are written that you may believe that Jesus is the Christ, the Son of God, and that by believing you may have life in his name" (John 20:30-31). Testimony would lead to faith, and faith to life. Indeed John seems to see his Gospel in terms of testimony to Christ. It is almost as if it is a kind of court scene in which Jesus is on trial and a succession of witnesses is called, beginning with John the Baptist.

1. What thoughts and feelings do you have as you read these five verses?

2. How is the Word identified with God (vv. 1-2)?

3. What is the significance of the fact that Christ was part of the creation of all things (v. 3)?

4. In what senses could the life of God be called "light" for all people (vv. 4-5)?

5. *Read John 1:6-9.* What is the work of John (not the Gospel writer but John the Baptist)?

6. Look back over verses 1-9. How do they express the universal nature of the light?

7. *Read John 1:10-14.* After such an ethereal introduction to the Word, what surprising paradox does the Gospel writer introduce (vv. 10-11)?

---

8. What extraordinary benefit is granted to those who believe in this Word (vv. 12-13)?

This Word of God, the perfect expression of the Father's being, one day "became flesh and made his dwelling among us" (v. 14). To him John bears witness. It is not a visitation but an incarnation. God becomes a human being in Jesus of Nazareth. The paradox is amazing. The Creator assumes the human frailty of his creatures. The Eternal One enters time. The all-powerful makes himself vulnerable. The all-holy exposes himself to temptation. And in the end the immortal dies.

---

9. What significance do you see in the fact that the Word "became flesh" (v. 14) rather than that he appeared like flesh or inhabited flesh?

---

10. How does the Gospel writer John verify his right to bear witness to the Word (v. 14)?

---

11. Christ came "full of grace and truth" (v. 14). What might be different if he had come with only grace?

If he had come with only truth?

Summary: I find it helpful to look in the four Evangelists for four dimensions of the saving purpose of God: its length, depth, breadth and height. Matthew reveals its length, for he depicts the Christ of Scripture who looks back over long centuries of expectation. Mark emphasizes its depth, for he depicts the Suffering Servant who looks down to the depths of the humiliation he endured. In Luke it is the breadth of God's purpose that emerges, for he depicts the Savior of the world who looks around in mercy to the broadest possible spectrum of human beings. Then John reveals its height, for he depicts the Word made flesh, who looks up to the heights from which he came and to which he intends to raise us. No wonder Paul prayed that with all God's people we might be able to "grasp how wide and long and high and deep is the love of Christ" (Ephesians 3:18)—dimensions that some of the early church fathers saw symbolized in the shape of the cross.

Apply————————————————————————

■ Consider the remarkable truth that God becomes a human being in Jesus Christ. How do you respond to that fact? (Does it still have power to amaze you? Is it so familiar to you that it has little impact?)

What reasons can you think of for God *not* to become a human being for our sake?

Christ, the incarnate Word, is also the life and light for all human beings. Where do you feel spiritual lifelessness?

Where do you need his light to shine? (Consider hidden areas of sin, decisions you must make, areas of confusion or bewilderment, uncertainties about the future, and any other areas where you need his light to overcome the darkness.)

Pray

■ Offer thanks to Jesus for becoming one of us. Pray that the fact of the incarnation will never seem ordinary to you. Ask him to shed his light on areas of darkness, uncertainty, fear and concealed sin. Praise him for bringing grace and bringing truth to your life and to the entire world. Pray for those who need to see his light and become children of God.

5
LIBERATOR

Galatians 3:1-14; 5:13-18

*T*hroughout this letter one senses Paul's hot indignation toward false teachers who are troubling the church by perverting the gospel (Galatians 1:7). So keenly does Paul feel the need to be loyal to the truth of the gospel that he is prepared even to have an embarrassing public confrontation with his fellow apostle Peter over it (Galatians 2:11-14). Probably the key text of Galatians is 5:1, where Paul writes, "It is for freedom that Christ has set us free. Stand firm, then, and do not let yourselves be burdened again by a yoke of slavery." Paul thus portrays Christ as the supreme liberator and portrays salvation in terms of freedom.

Open———————————————————————————

■ Consider this statement: *Freedom is the right to do anything you want to do, with no restrictions.* To what extent do you agree or disagree, and why?

Study———————————————————————————

■ *Read Galatians 3:1-9.* If Christ is the supreme liberator and salvation means freedom, we should inquire about the nature of this freedom.

1. What controversy was taking place in the Galatian churches concerning the heart of the gospel?

2. How does the life of Abraham verify that salvation is by faith and not by human effort?

3. Why is it "foolish" (3:1) to count on human effort for salvation?

4. Christian freedom is *freedom from the law.* Paul writes of "the curse of the law," meaning by this expression not the law itself but the judgment that the law pronounces on those who disobey it. *Read Galatians 3:10-14.* What responsibility falls on the person who tries to seek justification through keeping the law (3:10-12)?

5. How does Christ rescue us from the curse of the law (3:13-14)?

Summary: Christ takes our place, bears our curse and dies our death. No wonder Paul is determined to boast in nothing except the cross (Galatians 6:14).

6. *Read Galatians 5:13-15.* How can Christian freedom be misused?

7. How does Paul contradict the idea that *freedom* means doing whatever we want with no restrictions?

8. When have you experienced a sense of freedom in serving others?

Summary: Freedom from the law and its curse does not give us freedom to disobey the moral law or to indulge our sinful nature. On the contrary, Christian freedom is freedom to serve, not freedom to sin.

9. Christian freedom is also *freedom from the flesh,* from our fallen, self-indulgent nature. *Read Galatians 5:16-18.* What conflict goes on within each Christian believer?

10. What specific forms has this conflict taken in your own life?

11. What difference does the Holy Spirit make in this conflict?

Paul writes in Galatians that even those who have been justified by grace through faith in Christ are involved in an unrelenting conflict between the flesh (our fallen nature) and the Spirit (the indwelling Holy Spirit). The winner in this internal conflict depends on the attitude we adopt toward each. If we belong to Christ we have crucified (that is, radically repudiated) our sinful nature. We are to live by the Spirit, that is, follow the Spirit's promptings—for then the flesh will be subdued to the Spirit, and the fruit of the Spirit will ripen in our character.

Summary: Paul's witness to Christ the Liberator in Galatians is that by his cross we can be redeemed from the law's curse and that by his Spirit we can be delivered from the power of our fallen nature. As a result, we are no longer slaves but Abraham's children and the sons and daughters of God (Galatians 3:29; 4:7).

Apply

■ What efforts are you tempted to make in order to earn your own righteousness, rather than trusting in the righteousness of Christ?

When have you come to a particular realization that salvation is only through what Christ has done and not through keeping the law?

How have you experienced the Holy Spirit's help in overcoming sin?

What struggles with sin do you still experience?

Pray

■ Express your thanks to Christ the Liberator for taking all your sin on himself and dying for you. Thank him for freedom from the law and for freedom from the power of the sinful nature. Ask for the Spirit's continual help to follow his promptings.

6
COMING JUDGE

2 Thessalonians 2:1-17

*P*aul and his companions visit Thessalonica during his second mission-ary journey, and his first letter to them is evidently written and dispatched within months, even weeks, of his visit. And his second letter follows soon afterward. Both letters are addressed to some very new converts. Only recently have they "turned to God from idols to serve the living and true God" (1 Thessalonians 1:9). Although Paul has some immediate pur-poses for writing, the chief emphasis of the Thessalonian letters relates to the coming of Christ to save and to judge. Each of the eight chapters into which 1 and 2 Thessalonians have been divided contains a reference to the parousia (the return of Christ). As always, Paul is addressing pastoral problems that he knows only sound doctrine can solve.

Open
■ What do you think of when you hear the word *judgment?*

Study
■ *Read 2 Thessalonians 2:1-4.* Paul loved the Thessalonians as fathers and mothers love their children, and he was anxious to help those who were in special need.

1. What had "unsettled" and "alarmed" the Thessalonian Christians (vv. 1-2)?

2. How does Paul reassure them?

3. What does Paul say must happen before the Lord's return (vv. 3-4)?

4. *Read 2 Thessalonians 2:5-12.* How has Paul tried to prepare the people for this waiting period before Christ's return (vv. 5-6)?

5. What will characterize the time before Christ's return (vv. 7-12)?

6. How will the Lord Jesus deal with the forces that oppose him (v. 8)?

7. How much effort will it take for Jesus to destroy his opponents (v. 8)?

Summary: Some of the Thessalonian Christians are confused by a rumor that the day of the Lord has already come. Paul refutes this error by unfolding a Christian philosophy of history (vv. 1-12). The parousia (the coming of Christ) cannot take place, he explains, until the rebellion (the coming of Antichrist) occurs, and this rebellion will not happen until what is holding it back has been removed.

The identity of the restraining influence (v. 6), which is personalized in verse 7, has long occupied the minds of students. But the most probable reconstruction is that it refers to Rome and the power of the state. Indeed every state, being the official guardian of law and order, public peace and justice, is intended by God to restrain evil. Meanwhile, even during the period of restraint, and before the lawless one (Antichrist) is revealed, "the secret power of lawlessness is already at work" (v. 7). We detect its subversive influence in atheism, totalitarianism, materialism, moral relativism and social permissiveness. But one day secret subversion will become open rebellion, when the lawless one is revealed. Then we can expect a period (mercifully short) of political, social and moral chaos in which both God and law are impudently flouted, until suddenly the Lord Jesus will come and overthrow him.

8. *Read 2 Thessalonians 2:13-17.* Still writing in light of Christ's coming, how does Paul's tone change from the preceding passage?

9. What gives the Thessalonians hope to face Christ, the coming judge (vv. 13-14)?

10. What factors enable them to continue to live in hope as they wait for Christ's coming (vv. 15-17)?

11. When you think of Christ coming to judge the world, what gives you hope to be able to face him?

Summary: Here then are the three acts in the eschatological drama. Now is the time of *restraint,* in which lawlessness is being held in check. Next will come the time of *rebellion,* in which the control of the law will be removed and the lawless one will be revealed. Finally will come the time of *retribution,* in which the Lord Christ will defeat and destroy the Antichrist. This is God's program. Meanwhile the Thessalonians are to stand firm in the teaching they have previously received from the apostle. Whatever their troubles, Paul points them to the coming Christ.

Apply————————————————————
■ What are your feelings, expectations, hopes or even fears about Christ's return?

In what ways has your attitude toward Christ's return changed over the years, and why?

How do you identify with the believers Paul addressed in 2 Thessalonians 2:13-15?

Pray————————————————————
■ Pray 2 Thessalonians 2:16-17 for yourself and for others you know who need its encouragement.

7
SAVIOR

Romans 3:9-31

*D*uring Paul's third missionary journey, he spends two years in Corinth and three years in Ephesus. He is quite busy these five years with ministries of evangelism, apologetics and instruction, but Paul seems to have time for writing. It is in this period that he writes his letter to the Romans (whose material he may have tried out in the hall of Tyrannus) and his two surviving letters to Corinth. *Salvation* is their dominant theme.

Open

■ People often use the word *salvation* in ways that have nothing to do with sin or righteousness. For example: "The insurance money finally came through and it was our *salvation*." "When I was a senior in high school, we got a new guidance counselor and she was my *salvation*." "Moving to a healthier climate has been my *salvation*." What do people mean when they use the word *salvation* in those ways?

How do you think those usages compare or contrast with what the Bible means by *salvation?*

Study────────────────────────────────

1. *Read Romans 3:9-20.* At the start of the chapter, Paul was discussing whether there might be an "advantage" in being a Jew (v. 1). What assessment does Paul now make concerning the entire human race?

2. Paul seems to come to extreme conclusions about humanity, especially in his Old Testament quotations (vv. 10-18). Who do you think of when you read verses 10-18?

3. In what ways (if any) do you identify yourself in verses 10-18?

4. *Scan Romans 1:18—2:16.* Here is the background for Paul's question "What shall we conclude then?" in Romans 3:9. On what basis could Paul say that outwardly good, moral, upright people are also under God's condemnation?

5. What is the value of the law according to 3:19-20?

In Romans, after a brief introduction that focuses on Christ (Romans 1:1-5), the universal need for salvation is powerfully set forth. First depraved pagans, next critical moralizers and then self-confident Jews are arraigned, until the whole human race is found guilty and inexcusable (Romans 1:18—3:20).

6. *Read Romans 3:21-31.* Paul paints a dark, gloomy and pessimistic picture of humanity. How would you describe the difference in mood that he introduces with verse 21?

7. In what ways are human beings equal according to verses 22-24 and verses 29-31?

8. How did Christ accomplish the forgiveness of sins (vv. 24-26)?

9. What contrasts do you find between righteousness through keeping the law and righteousness through Christ (vv. 19-26)?

10. Why do Christian believers have no grounds for boasting (vv. 27-28)?

11. How do verses 21-26 demonstrate the justice of God?

12. How do verses 21-26 demonstrate the mercy of God?

"But now," Paul continues with a mighty adversative, "a righteousness from God" (that is, God's righteous way of making righteous the unrighteous) has been revealed in the gospel, to be received by faith alone. In consequence, having been justified by faith, we enjoy peace with God, we are standing in grace, and we rejoice in the prospect of sharing God's glory (Romans 5:1-11). Two humanities have now been portrayed, one characterized by sin and guilt, the other by grace and faith.

Summary: Romans is the New Testament's most thorough exposition of salvation, describing its need, its nature and its means; indicating its radical implications in the new multiracial community; and celebrating Jesus Christ crucified, risen, reigning and coming as the only Savior.

Apply————————————————
■ How do you respond personally to the idea that no one, no matter how morally respectable, is righteous in God's sight?

Paul wrote that our boasting is "excluded" because Christ justifies us freely by his grace. What reasons are you tempted to find for boasting in your own goodness?

What practical reminders can you provide for yourself that your salvation is by faith in Christ alone?

Pray————————————————
■ Offer thanks and praise to Jesus the Savior for his free forgiveness. Confess areas where you are self-righteous or look down on others who seem more sinful.

8
VICTOR

1 Corinthians 15:1-28

P aul's first letter to the Corinthians is about the same length as his letter to the Romans, but its contents are very different. Romans is an orderly, carefully constructed exposition of the gospel, whereas 1 Corinthians handles an assortment of as many as twenty diverse themes, in which Paul is responding either to pastoral needs he perceives in Corinth or to questions the Corinthians have put to him. The letter begins with the factions that are tearing the Corinthian church apart. By contrast, 1 Corinthians 15 (its last main chapter apart from personal messages) is a magnificent exposition of the gospel that, more than anything else, is calculated to unify the church.

Open

■ What do you think would be different today if Christ had not been raised from the dead?

Study

■ *Read 1 Corinthians 15:1-11.* Paul says he wants to remind the Corinthians of the gospel, which he assumes is a universally recognizable message. He himself proclaimed it to them, and they have received it.

More, they have taken their stand on it. And they are being saved by it, so long as they are holding firm to it, since otherwise they would have believed in vain.

---

1. What is the essence of this gospel (vv. 1-4)?

---

2. What is the significance of the many appearances of the resurrected Christ to various people (vv. 5-8)?

---

3. How is the grace of God displayed in Paul's life (vv. 9-11)?

Paul moves directly from "he appeared to me also" (v. 8) to "I am the least of the apostles" (v. 9), for a resurrection appearance by Christ is an indispensable qualification for apostleship (see Acts 1:21-22, 25; 1 Corinthians 9:1). Having given his list of appearances, Paul now concludes with an important statement about the gospel (v. 11): "Whether, then, it was I or they, this is what we preach, and this is what you believed." It is a claim to the unity both of the apostles' proclamation and of the church's faith, alongside their diverse gifts.

---

4. *Read 1 Corinthians 15:12-19.* What false teaching is apparently going around in Corinth (v. 12)?

---

5. What does this false teaching imply about Jesus Christ (v. 13)?

6. If the teaching were true, what other terrible things would also be true (vv. 14-19)?

7. How would your life be different if you weren't able to live in the hope of Christ?

8. *Read 1 Corinthians 15:20-28.* In complete contrast to the false teaching Paul writes about in verses 12-19, "Christ has indeed been raised from the dead" (v. 20)! In what sense is Christ the "firstfruits" (vv. 20, 23)?

9. What victories still remain for Christ to win (vv. 24-26)?

10. How will the Son show his obedience to the Father even at the end of time (vv. 27-28)?

Summary: Of first importance in the gospel are four events: the death, burial, resurrection and appearances of the Lord Jesus. These four events are not of equal importance. Of supreme importance, as we know from repeated references in the New Testament, are the death and resurrection of Jesus; the importance of the burial and the appearances is in relation to these. Thus Christ died for our sins according to the Scriptures and then was buried to demonstrate the reality of his death. Next, Christ was raised on the third day according to the Scriptures and then appeared and was seen, to demonstrate the reality of his resurrection.

Apply

■ All Christians think about Christ's resurrection at Easter. Are there other times of the year when you especially think about it?

In what sense has Christ showed himself as the Victor for you or for others you know?

In what outward circumstances do you still long to see the victory of Christ?

In what internal struggles do you still long to see the victory of Christ?

Pray

■ Thank the Lord for his victory over sin and over all evil forces. Pray that you will always be a participant in his victory. Thank him for his victory even over death, the final enemy.

9
SUPREME LORD

Ephesians 1:15-23

*P*aul is incarcerated several times as "a prisoner for the Lord." It seems reasonable to conjecture that while in prison, delivered from the feverish activity of his missionary lifestyle, Paul has extra time in which to meditate. Prison bars can confine Paul's body but not his soul. It seems that during these years, although he can neither evangelize more cities nor visit the churches, his mind soars into heaven. Conviction about the Lord Jesus, highly exalted yet simultaneously near, dominates Paul's prison letters.

Open
■ Consider the question "Who's in charge here?" What are some answers you would expect to hear? Which answers are you inclined to believe?

Study
■ *Read Ephesians 1:15-19.* While Ephesians offers us a glorious picture of participating with Christ in the heavenly realms, it is also known for its down-to-earth exhortations. We look, on one hand, at the church, God's new society, whose unity, truth and holiness Paul describes, and

on the other at the family or household, where our new life demands new relationships.

---

1. "For this reason" (v. 15) refers to Ephesians 1:1-14, where Paul writes that, in the purposes of God, believers have been chosen, redeemed and marked with the Holy Spirit. What does Paul continually pray for the Ephesians (vv. 15-19)?

---

2. List the spiritual blessings Paul prays for in verses 17-19.

How would they equip believers to live in a hostile world?

---

3. Which of Paul's prayers would you like to know that someone is praying for you right now?

---

4. Describe someone that you think has "The Spirit of wisdom and revelation" (v. 17).

---

5. What does it mean to have "the eyes of your heart enlightened" (v. 18)?

6. *Read Ephesians 1:19-23.* How would you picture the scene in verses 20-21?

7. What authority does the risen Christ have on Earth (vv. 22-23)?

8. Christ is seated far above all conceivable rivals (v. 21). What are some of the "rivals" to Christ around us today?

9. According to verses 22-23, what is our involvement in Christ's rule over all things?

10. As you look around, what appears to be *not* under the feet of Christ in the world at large?

in your community?

in your church fellowship?

Summary: The perspective is almost overwhelming, as Jesus is seen to be the supreme head of both creations: the universe and the church. But there is something more. The death and resurrection of Jesus Christ are not only objective, saving events but they are also realities that we can personally participate in.

Apply————————————————————————

■ For you personally, what is the most reassuring element of this Scripture passage, and why?

———————————————————————————————

How has Christ shown himself to be the Supreme Lord in your life circumstances?

———————————————————————————————

What destructive influences, temptations or struggles—in the world at large, in your community, in your church or in yourself—do you need to see as already under the feet of Christ?

Pray————————————————————————

■ Pray Paul's prayer in Ephesians 1:17-19 for yourself and for others as God brings them to mind.

10
HEAD OF THE CHURCH

2 Timothy 1:8-14; 2:8-13

*I*n all three pastoral letters (1-2 Timothy and Titus) Paul's overriding preoccupation is the church. Christ died "to purify for himself a people" (Titus 2:14). Consequently, Paul is concerned with the life of the local church and particularly with the church's responsibility to guard and teach the truth. The church is "the pillar and foundation of the truth" (1 Timothy 3:15); its foundation to hold it firm and its pillar to thrust it high.

Open

■ What does it mean to be faithful to someone?

Who stands out to you as an example of faithfulness?

Study

■ *Read 2 Timothy 1:8-14.* The second letter to Timothy seems to have been written from prison shortly before Paul is executed. It is probably the most intimate and affectionate of all Paul's letters.

1. Imagine that you are Timothy and have received this letter from Paul. You realize that it is probably the last message you will receive from him. He has been like a father to you (see 2 Timothy 1:2; 2:1). What thoughts and feelings would you experience?

2. What things are named in verses 8-10 that Christ has done independent of any human action or initiative?

3. Why is Paul able to endure suffering for the gospel?

4. In 2 Timothy 1:8 and 12, Paul rejects the idea of being ashamed of Christ. What might tempt a Christian to be ashamed of identifying with Christ?

5. What does Paul encourage Timothy to continue to do (1:13-14)?

6. Paul uses the word *entrusted* twice (1:12, 14). In each case what has been entrusted, and who is it entrusted to?

Knowing that his own death is approaching, Paul exhorts Timothy not to be ashamed of Christ but to be conscientious in his life and ministry, to cling in difficult times both to the Old Testament Scriptures and to the apostles' teaching, and to preach the Word.

---

7. *Read 2 Timothy 2:8-13.* Verse 9 is the second time Paul refers to his suffering for the gospel (see also 2 Timothy 1:8). What inspires Paul to endure such unfair suffering (2:8-10)?

---

8. In these verses Paul describes an all-powerful, ever-faithful Christ who is certainly worthy of all worship. Why would anyone have to suffer for preaching about this Christ?

---

9. Paul refers to 2 Timothy 2:11-13 as "a trustworthy saying." What makes these words trustworthy?

---

10. What hopes are contained in 2 Timothy 2:11-13?

---

11. What cautions are contained in 2 Timothy 2:11-13?

Summary: Perhaps the text that best sums up the main message of all three of Paul's pastoral letters is 2 Timothy 2:2, "The things you have heard me say in the presence of many witnesses entrust to reliable men who will also be qualified to teach others." Nothing is more necessary for the life, health and growth of the church than the faithful teaching of the truth.

Apply————————————————————————

■ When has Christ shown himself to be faithful to you, despite your unfaithfulness?

Under what circumstances are you tempted to be ashamed of Christ?

What have you entrusted to Christ?

What has Christ entrusted to you?

Pray————————————————————————

■ Thank the Lord for his faithfulness. Pray for courage and boldness so that you will never be ashamed of the gospel.

11
MORAL TEACHER

James 1:19-27

*J*ames is one of the Lord's brothers, who, though unbelieving during Jesus' lifetime, seems to have come to faith through a resurrection appearance. He later becomes the acknowledged leader of the Jerusalem church and of Jewish Christians. What sort of witness, then, does James bear to Jesus? "Very little," some will reply. And it is true that Jesus is named only twice in the book of James. But, indirectly, James bears witness to Jesus throughout. For one of the most interesting features of his letter is the number of times he alludes in a clear way to the recorded teaching of Jesus and specifically to his Sermon on the Mount, as if he had been present and heard it—which is not impossible. It is indisputable that James presents Jesus as essentially a moral teacher.

Open

■ If you had to express the essence of Christian morality in one sentence, what would you say?

Study

1. *Read James 1:19-27.* How does what James writes compare with what you know of Christ's teachings?

2. What problems are avoided by being "quick to listen, slow to speak and slow to become angry" (v. 19)?

3. Surely God is angry at sin. Then why do you think James put anger and righteousness in opposition to each other (v. 20)?

4. James says to "get rid of all moral filth and . . . evil" and "humbly accept the word planted in you" (v. 21). Why are evil and humility in opposition to each other?

5. How does James use a mirror to demonstrate obedience or lack of obedience (vv. 22-25)?

6. When God's Word shows you that you have sinned, what is your first reaction?

7. What promise is given to the one who obeys the Word (v. 25)?

8. According to James, what one practice negates a person's profession of religion (v. 26)?

9. Why do you think this one practice is so destructive?

10. James sets forth several actions that demonstrate "pure and fault-less" religion in the sight of God (v. 27). How do those actions charac-terize the life that Christ lived on Earth?

Summary: Here is our threefold ethical duty to ourselves, to our neigh-bor and to our God. Tongue control is an index of self-control. The care of widows and orphans is an example of neighbor love. Keeping oneself unstained by the world is the negative counterpart to giving God the worship due to his name. While Paul stressed the faith that issues in works, James stresses the works that issue from faith.

Apply

■ What parts of God's Word do you tend to read and then forget or ignore (as in vv. 23-24)?

How has obedience to the Word brought you freedom (v. 25)?

By the standard of verses 26-27, how would you rate your religious faith?

Pray

■ Ask God to show you where you need to speak less and listen more. Pray about the things that anger you. Thank God for his perfect law and for his forgiveness for every sin and failure.

12
GREAT HIGH PRIEST

Hebrews 9:11-28

*T*he letter to the Hebrews is anonymous. Nevertheless, although the author's identity is uncertain, his purpose is not. He is writing his letter or treatise to a local church of Hebrew Christians, perhaps in or near Jerusalem, who are in danger of relapsing into Judaism. The author hopes to establish them in Christ by demonstrating Christ's finality. Exposed to vicious persecution and specious argument, they are wavering in their Christian faith and are contemplating apostasy to Judaism. If only they could grasp the absolute finality of Jesus Christ, it is inconceivable that they would drift back. The eternity of our final and perfect salvation fills the writer's mind.

Open————————————————————
■ List some things which are *once and for all*.

Why is *once and for all* comparatively rare?

Study

■ *Read Hebrews 9:11-15.* After an introduction, the author of Hebrews moves toward his first great theme, which is the superiority of the priesthood of Christ. The old Levitical priests had to be continuously replaced, because death prevented them from continuing in office, but Jesus holds his priesthood permanently because he lives forever.

1. What were the elements of the sacrifices that Jewish priests made in the earthly tabernacle?

2. How is Christ's sacrifice radically different from the old sacrifices?

3. What does Christ's sacrifice achieve for us that the old sacrifices could never achieve (vv. 14-15)?

Having established the final supremacy of the priesthood of Jesus, the author comes to the achievement of his sacrifice. A priest had to have something to offer, so what, then, did Jesus have to offer? The answer is his own blood—that is, himself: he laid down in violent death. He is the victim as well as the priest, and the author explains the superiority of his sacrifice.

4. *Read Hebrews 9:16-22.* After he had communicated God's commandments to the people, how did Moses confirm the covenant that was being made (vv. 19-21)?

5. Why was blood a necessary part of the old covenant (vv. 16-18, 22)?

6. *Read Hebrews 9:23-28.* What are the two sanctuaries and how do they differ (vv. 23-24)?

7. Why does Christ's sacrifice never have to be repeated (vv. 25-26)?

8. Because of Christ's sacrifice, what is our eager anticipation (vv. 27-28)?

9. Once we have grasped the finality of Christ's priesthood, sacrifice and covenant, it seems that we could not contemplate any alternative. Yet we sometimes live as though Christ did not do enough and we still need more. How have you seen people fall into the error that, in order to reach God, they need Christ plus something else? (For example, Christ plus the teachings of a popular speaker or writer.)

Summary: Point by point, the author of Hebrews shows Christ fulfilling the Old Testament's imperfect ritual.

☐ Only the high priest might enter the holy of holies, but Jesus secured access into God's presence for all his people.

☐ Only once a year (on the Day of Atonement) might the high priest enter, but Jesus secured for us continuous access.

□ Only with the blood of animal sacrifice might the high priest enter, but Jesus entered with his own blood.

□ Only cleansing from ceremonial defilement was secured by the Old Testament sacrifices, but Jesus secured the forgiveness of our sins.

□ Only by regular sacrifices could the people remain clean, but Jesus died once and for all.

Apply————————————————————————————

■ Meditate on each point in the summary section above, consider how Jesus not only is superior to other priests but is our supreme High Priest who mediates between us and God the Father.

How do you tend to try to add on to Christ, as though his life and death are not sufficient?

What one statement or phrase in Hebrews 9:11-28 speaks to you most powerfully about the sufficiency of Christ, your Great High Priest?

Pray ————————————————————————————

■ "Since we have confidence to enter the Most Holy Place by the blood of Jesus, by a new and living way opened for us through the curtain, that is, his body, and since we have a great priest over the house of God, let us draw near to God with a sincere heart in full assurance of faith, having our hearts sprinkled to cleanse us from a guilty conscience and having our bodies washed with pure water" (Hebrews 10:19-22). Take this promise personally. Trusting in what our High Priest has done for you, draw near to God and pray humbly but boldly for yourself and others.

13
MODEL IN SUFFERING

1 Peter 2:18-25

*P*eter had been entrusted with the task of preaching the gospel to the Jews (Galatians 2:7), and it seems clear that in his first letter he has Jewish readers principally (though not exclusively) in mind. Peter's opening doxology praises God that he has given us a new birth into a living hope through the resurrection of Jesus Christ (1 Peter 1:3). And this living hope sustains us, however fierce the opposition may be. Although Peter handles many other topics in his first letter, his main emphasis is on Christian behavior in the face of persecution. The words *suffer* and *suffering* occur seven times in relation to Christ and nine times in relation to Christians.

Open———————————————————————————
■ Think about people you know who have suffered or are suffering. Describe someone who is a model for you.

Study———————————————————————————
■ *Read 1 Peter 2:18-25.* Peter is writing to believers dispersed throughout the pagan Roman Empire (1 Peter 1:1) in a context where slavery is ingrained in the culture. This paragraph relates particularly to Christian slaves whose masters are not considerate but harsh.

1. What would give the slaves endurance under unjust suffering (vv. 18-19)?

2. What contrast does Peter draw between suffering justly as punishment for doing wrong and suffering unjustly for doing good (v. 20)?

3. Reflect on verse 21. What larger principle about the Christian life is Peter illustrating with his instructions to slaves?

1 Peter 1:6-7 teaches that as we endure all kinds of trials we must remember that suffering tests, strengthens and purifies faith, as fire does gold. This will result in glory to God when Jesus Christ is revealed.

4. Consider a time that you experienced suffering because of your Christian faith. What was your immediate reaction?

5. How did Christ behave under unjust suffering (vv. 22-24)?

6. Where did Christ place his trust when he was falsely accused (v. 23)?

7. To what extent has the example of Christ helped you when you are insulted or unfairly accused because of your identity with him?

8. What has been the outcome of Christ's acceptance of suffering (vv. 24-25)?

9. We have a Shepherd and Overseer of our souls (v. 25). What are the implications of that fact when we are falsely accused or insulted in any way for the name of Christ?

Summary: What is the Christian's attitude to undeserved suffering? Peter makes it clear that Christians are not to retaliate. But he goes further than that. His first letter contains six passages on suffering. Each expresses a different admonition, and each points his readers to Christ. We must bear unjust suffering because suffering is part of the Christian's calling. Christ has left us an example of nonretaliation so that we might follow in his steps.

Apply————————————————————

■ In what circumstances are you likely to retaliate against someone who has hurt you?

When you are unfairly accused of anything, what may keep you from following Christ's example of simply trusting God?

What has been the long-term effect of suffering on your spiritual maturity?

Pray————————————————————

■ Pray about every situation where you feel unfairly put upon, ridiculed or blamed, especially when the abuse is coming because you are a Christian. Confess your tendency to justify yourself or to trust in anything or anyone but the Lord. Commit these difficult circumstances to God, and resolve not to retaliate but to let him deal with your accusers. Thank him for being the Shepherd and Overseer of your soul.

Guidelines for Leaders

My grace is sufficient for you. (2 Corinthians 12:9)

If leading a small group is something new for you, don't worry. These sessions are designed to be led easily. Because the Bible study questions flow from observation to interpretation to application, you may feel as if the studies lead themselves.

You don't need to be an expert on the Bible or a trained teacher to lead a small group discussion. As a leader, you can guide group members to discover for themselves what the Bible has to say and to listen for God's guidance. This method of learning will allow group members to remember much more of what is said than a lecture would.

This study guide is flexible. You can use it with a variety of groups—students, professionals, neighborhood or church groups. Each study takes forty-five to sixty minutes in a group setting.

There are some important facts to know about group dynamics and encouraging discussion. The suggestions listed below should equip you to effectively and enjoyably fulfill your role as leader.

Preparing for the Study

1. Ask God to help you understand and apply the passage in your own life. Unless this happens, you will not be prepared to lead others. Pray too for the various members of the group. Ask God to open your hearts to the message of his Word and motivate you to action.

2. Read the introduction to the entire guide to get an overview of the topics that will be explored.

3. As you begin each study, read and reread the assigned Bible passage to familiarize yourself with it.

4. This study guide is based on the New International Version of the Bible. It will help you and the group if you use this translation as the basis for your study and discussion.

5. Carefully work through each question in the study. Spend time in meditation and reflection as you consider how to respond.

6. Write your thoughts and responses in the space provided in the study guide. This will help you to express your understanding of the passage clearly.

7. It may help to have a Bible dictionary handy. Use it to look up any unfamiliar words, names or places. (For additional help on how to study a passage, see *How to Lead a LifeGuide Bible Study* from InterVarsity Press, USA.)

8. Take the "Apply" portion of each study seriously. Consider how you need to apply the Scripture to your life. Remember that the group members will follow your lead in responding to the studies. They will not go any deeper than you do.

Leading the Study

1. Begin the study on time. Open with prayer, asking God to help the group to understand and apply the passage.

2. Be sure that everyone in your group has a study guide. Encourage the group to prepare beforehand for each discussion by reading the introduction to the guide and by working through the questions in each study.

3. At the beginning of your first time together, explain that these studies are meant to be discussions, not lectures. Encourage the members of the group to participate. However, do not put pressure on those who may be hesitant to speak during the first few sessions.

4. Have a group member read aloud the introduction at the beginning of the discussion.

5. Every session begins with an "open" question, which is meant to be asked before the passage is read. These questions are designed to introduce the theme of the study and encourage group members to begin to open up. Encourage as many members as possible to participate, and be ready to get the discussion going with your own response. These opening questions can reveal where our thoughts or feelings need to be transformed by Scripture. That is why it is especially important not to read the passage before the question is asked. The passage will tend to color the honest reactions people would otherwise give because they are, of course, supposed to think the way the Bible does.

6. Have a group member read aloud the passage to be studied.

7. As you ask the study questions, keep in mind that they are designed to be used just as they are written. You may simply read them aloud. Or you may prefer to express them in your own words.

There may be times when it is appropriate to deviate from the study guide. For example, a question may have already been answered. If so, move on to the next question. Or someone may raise an important question not covered in the guide. Take time to discuss it, but try to keep the group from going off on tangents.

8. Avoid answering your own questions. If necessary repeat or rephrase them until they are clearly understood. Or point the group to the commentary woven into the guide to clarify the context or meaning *without answering the question*. An eager group quickly becomes passive and silent if members think the leader will do most of the talking.

9. Don't be afraid of silence in response to the discussion questions. People may need time to think about the question before formulating their answers.

10. Don't be content with just one answer. Ask, "What do the rest of you think?" or "Anything else?" until several people have given answers to the question.

11. Acknowledge all contributions. Try to be affirming whenever possible. Never reject an answer. If it is clearly off-base, ask, "Which verse led you to that conclusion?" or again, "What do the rest of you think?"

12. Don't expect every answer to be addressed to you, even though this will probably happen at first. As group members become more at ease, they will begin to truly interact with each other. This is one sign of healthy discussion.

13. Don't be afraid of controversy. It can be very stimulating. If you don't resolve an issue completely, don't be frustrated. Explain that the group will move on and God may enlighten all of you in later sessions.

14. Periodically summarize what the group has said about the passage. This helps to draw together the various ideas mentioned and gives continuity to the study. But don't preach.

15. Conclude your time together with conversational prayer, adapting the prayer suggestion at the end of the study to your group. Ask for God's help in following through on the commitments you've made.

16. End on time.

Many more suggestions and helps can be found in *How to Lead a LifeGuide Bible Study* and *The Big Book on Small Groups* (both from InterVarsity Press, USA) or *Housegroups* (Crossway Books UK). Reading through one of these books would be worth your time.